Muscle and a Shovel

Bible Class Teacher's Manual
13 Week Quarter

Michael J. Shank

Edited by Christa Bryant
Cover by Joe Kelly
Authored by Michael Shank
All credit and glory to God, Jesus Christ, and Randall
www.muscleandashovel.com

ISBN 10: 0692259546
ISBN 13: 978-0-692-25954-2

NOTE: Chapter titles are included in this workbook, but were removed from Revision 6. The intent is to prevent the reader from scanning the book and selectively reading a few chapters. This causes the lost to prejudge the story, and often prevents them from reading the book from beginning to end as intended.

It would be a great tragedy not to recognize that the one, true Creator, our God and Father in Heaven, has blessed this humble work beyond our wildest imaginations (Eph. 3:20). I cannot accept a shred of credit. Over ten thousand baptisms have resulted by God's hand through *Muscle and a Shovel* with an incalculable number of restorations and those proclaiming a renewed and deeper commitment to the Lord and His Cause. Therefore, the Shank family gives God the entirety of credit, honor, and glory for His hand of blessing on *Muscle and a Shovel.*

We know that we are nothing and that all our works are, as the Spirit so eloquently penned through Isaiah the Prophet, *as an unclean thing, and all our righteousness are as filthy rags; and we all do fade as a leaf; and our iniquities, like the wind, have taken us away* (Isaiah 64:6).

This Bible class workbook is based on the book which bears its name, and it is designed for perfecting and equipping you for the work of ministry (service) and for the edifying of the body of Christ (Ephesians 4:12).

I hope that you will find the contents to be useful, encouraging for your faith, inspiring a deeper commitment to Jesus Christ, and giving you the tools to become the type of courageous Christian seen so prevalently in the New Testament.

The Second Restoration cannot and will not begin, nor will it succeed, without **you**. **You** are the key. **You** are the soldier of Jesus Christ (Ephesians 6:10-11). **You** have a mission, and it is a mission second to none, to save that which was lost (Matthew 18:11), and to carry forward the work of our Master. And your weapon? The greatest and most powerful sword that has ever or will ever exist – the word of God (Ephesians 6:17).

Humbly in Him Who Died for Us,

Michael Shank

Make this workbook yours. Write in and all over it. Customize it in your own personal way to make it a tool that serves you well. Wear this thing out in your endeavor to reach the lost and dying world!

Objectives of this Course

TEACHER: There are three keys to follow so that you can guide your student toward getting the most out of this course. They are the notecards, action points, and discussion topics.

Bible memorization is the foundation of this course. Your encouragement to your students to complete the simple memorization drills in this lesson is most vital.

Action points are meant to be practical homework assignments that will foster spiritual growth and build confidence in your students.

Discussion is the meat of the course. You, as a teacher, should foster an environment of open discussion. Bible students learn from you, but also learn a great deal from others.

As you scan through this workbook, you will see that it the workbook is easily modified to teach a course that lasts beyond the traditional 13 week quarter. If you choose you have the opportunity to customize the timetable that best fits your class goals. The design was created with you in mind. The workbook can easily be modified to cover up to 44 weeks, or it can fit within the traditional 13 week course model. It's all up to you. May our God give you, the teacher, great wisdom, patience, love, and zeal for the work.

Teacher instructions and answers are always found in brackets [ ].

The class objective, if designed by the framework of this workbook, is to equip you, the Christian, for a future of greater confidence in reaching out to the lost with the gospel of Jesus Christ. With this aim in mind, please know that this book is not like the traditional class workbook you have probably used in the past.

You will find that this workbook is filled with scripture, but it is formatted in a way that attempts to focus your class activity on class discussion, rather than using the customary "fill in the blank" format.

Below you will find the optimal way to use this workbook listed in the order of importance.

1. **NOTECARDS.** For the Bible to be a lamp unto your feet and a light unto your path, the Word *must* be internalized. When you see this symbol, write the verse on a notecard.

2. **ACTION POINTS.** These are simple, practical, real-life things to work on during the week, whenever your schedule permits. When you see this symbol, it is an action for the week.

3. **DISCUSSION.** Learning Randall's methods should be fun, and the discussion sections should foster lively group discussions that are both instructive and enjoyable.

I hope that you will enjoy this class. Forty chapters and an epilogue is an enormous amount of material to try to cram into a thirteen-week time frame, so please forgive me for pushing you. And if you cannot cover it all in the time you have, don't fret! There is no deadline on spiritual growth. Have fun, learn, and reach out!

Week I: Chapters 1-4

You grin at the sense of pride and accomplishment you feel when looking at the arrows positioned exactly sixty feet from your left foot. Both arrows appear to be in the tiny yellow elliptical at the center of the field round – the coveted bull's-eye. From where you stand the arrows appear to be so close together that the fletchings are meshed together; the shaft of your last arrow is still vibrating slightly from the impact.

Those standing close gently pat you on the back. While those watching from the gallery clap loudly in reaction to your skills, hard work, dedication, and composure under pressure.

Field judges lift the target and begin walking it to you while family and friends engage you in excited accolades. As you hug a dear friend, volumous gasps come from the gallery; something is wrong! You turn quickly to the audience only to see that they are staring at something. They are staring at your target. The target that was carried to your shooting post by the judges. Your arrows are at the outer edge of the target, not even within any of the point rings.

How could this be? Didn't you see those two arrows positioned perfectly in the center? Didn't the crowd see the same with cheers and clapping? Didn't everyone think you had hit the bull's-eye? The reality puts you into shock, disappointment, frustration, and bewilderment. How could you have been so wrong?

Dennis, a dear friend and brother in Christ, said to me, "Michael, everyone thinks that they've hit the religious bull's-eye." A statement so simple, yet so profound. Everyone *thinks* they have hit the bull's-eye – *everyone*!

Why does *Muscle and a Shovel* incite such primal emotion? Why do so many love the story and react so positively – even to the point of obeying the gospel of Christ - while so many others react with intense indignance? Shock. It is complete shock to the system. Everyone thinks they have hit the bull's-eye, but when someone carries the target to their feet, and they are forced to realize that they have not even been close to the bull's-eye, it creates deep shock, terror, frustration, and perplexity.

Don't you think *you have* hit the biblical bull's-eye? Can you now understand how good-hearted, God-fearing, Jesus Christ believing, moral, hard-working, do-the-right-thing religious people feel when presented with evidence that confirms that they have not hit the bull's-eye?

Yes, it is easier to believe a lie heard a thousand times than to believe a fact one has never before heard. Throughout this lesson we will examine Randall, his approaches, his responses, and the attributes that fostered his attitude of gentle, persistent love. We will also study Mr. Mike's attitude, his emotional responses, and the reasons why he believed the things he believed.

We will cover the host of objections Mr. Mike offered to refute the Truth, and you will find the tools, the methods, and the attitudes to spread the gospel message with greater comfort and confidence than ever before.

You will need your Bible, a notepad, a stack of 3x5" index cards, a highlighter, and a box of Krispy Kreme doughnuts! Let's get started with a heartfelt prayer to our Father in Heaven:

"Dear Father in Heaven, we are so grateful for the precious gift of your Son's blood, and for the written Word. As we study this text with our Bible, please bless us with renewed zeal for the lost around us. In Christ's name, Amen."

(In Class: Spend approximately 10 minutes per chapter; 4 chapters per week.)

Chapter 1: Top of the Steps
March 15, 1988, 12:45 A.M.

 Acts 22:16

 ACTION POINTS

1. Write out your conversion story on paper. Do not minimize the importance of this exercise. We see the example of Paul sharing his conversion story. Read Acts 21:27 thru Acts 22:16.

2. Highlight the areas of your conversion where you can see that God's Divine Providence played a role.

3. In light of those who attended Michael and Jonetta's baptism, we can see that they were unrestrained in their singing and praying. Research the New Testament to find three significant portions of scripture that demonstrate how Christians were not ashamed of their faith, nor were they restrained from their joy.

DISCUSSION

1. Pick someone to tell their conversion story to the class. Telling their story will do several powerful things for the life and faith of the class:

   a. By sharing a story with the group, you are forced to recall the details, the people that influenced you, and your emotional/spiritual state prior to your immersion.

   b. Giving your story a voice encourages *every* hearer.

   c. Wisdom will be gleaned from your story as there are factors in your story that others will be able to relate.

   d. This exercise fosters confidence and courage within you.

2. Why was there an urgency in Michael and Jonetta to get baptized immediately?

   a. Regarding your conversion, was there an urgency for you to get to the burial ground (water)?

3. What shift occurred in Michael's mind when the cop confessed that he was a Christian? [providence of God]

   a. The concept of Divine __[Providence]__? Find three examples of this concept in the scriptures:

      1) __[Gen. 22:8; Gen. 30:30; Neh. 9:21]__

      2) __[Psa. 3:5; Matt. 10:9; 14:19-21]__

      3) __[Rom. 8:28; Col. 1:16-17]__

4. After reading about the men's singing while Michael and Jonetta changed into their baptismal garments, what would you say about the men's hearts? Why was Mike concerned about the time and thinking that their loud singing would wake up the neighbors? [worldliness, spiritual immaturity, carnal embarrassment]

5. Ask yourself the following:

    a. Should immersion into Christ be urgent?

    b. How would I react if I received a phone call in the middle of the night to come to the building to witness a baptism?

    c. Are we sometimes too reserved in our singing? In other words, are we sometimes *too* concerned about our singing skills or our personal performance? [Are we ashamed or embarrassed?]

Chapter 2:
An Unexpected Friendship

August 3, 1987, 7 Months Earlier

 Acts 20:28

 ACTION POINTS

1. On a notecard, make a list of ten people in your sphere of influence who are not members of the body of Christ, His blood-bought church (Acts 20:28). Do not "prejudge," just make the list. Keep this list with your verse notecards.

2. Pray for these people.

3. Pray that God will bless you with courage, wisdom, and an opportunity to "have something better for them a little later."

4. Research your New Testament, and find three instances of a Christian engaging the lost in a one-on-one situation.

    a. Instance 1: _[Acts 8:30]_

    b. Instance 2: _[Acts 16:23]_

    c. Instance 3: _[Acts 18:26]_

5. How can these three instances help to equip you in the future?

💬 DISCUSSION

1. What is revealed about Michael that demonstrates his "worldliness?" [returned the "Hollywood Howdy," his materialistic goals, his arrogance] (Worldliness Verse)  [Eph. 2:2]

2. "There was that guy again!" What were some of the personality traits that Randall demonstrated at the beginning of his introduction with Michael?

3. In your opinion, did Randall plan or premeditate his introduction to Michael?

4. Did Randall's attitude and/or appearance have an impact on Mike? What were the visible attributes of Randall's attitude and character?

5. Randall shifted the relationship immediately after introducing himself. How did he do this? ["Since you are my new friend, I'm going to give you something."]

6. After Randall's "shift" of conversation, what critical and bold move did Randall make? [gift of doughnuts in combination with his statement, "I might even have something better for you a little later!"]

7. Did Randall seem prepared?

8. If yes, how so? [2 Tim. 4:2; 1 Pet. 3:15]

9. Do you think that Randall had been praying for opportunities to seek and save the lost?

10. Do you think that Mr. Mike was the only person that Randall was focusing on? [Later in the story we find that Mike was not the only person Randall was focusing on.]

11. What can *you* do to be more prepared to engage someone in a spiritual conversation? [It begins with memorizing and internalizing the Word followed by prayer for opportunities.]

12. Discuss anything from your last week's action points.

Chapter 3:
Are They Nuts or What?

November 20, 1987

 Matthew 24:36

 ACTION POINTS

1. List three ways the Adversary has hindered your Christian growth. Have you been able to overcome these hindrances?

2. List three things that you can do this week that will help you to prepare to interest a lost soul in a Bible discussion.

   a. _____

   b. _____

   c. _____

3. Research four passages in the Old and New Testaments on patience and persistence.

   a. _____

   b. _____

   c. _____

   d. _____

 **DISCUSSION**

1. How long did Randall and Mike develop their friendship to this point in the story? [Approximately 3 ½ months]

2. What did Randall persistently do in his interactions with Mike? [Asked spiritual questions rather than preaching Bible facts]

3. Why did Mike think that Randall was "a very different sort of Christian?" [He lived what he believed and his knowledge of the Bible]

4. As a Christian, how do people see you? What is their "spiritual" perception of you?

5. What question did Randall ask Mike to open this day's spiritual dialogue? [How many times did you eat today?]

6. What portion of scripture did he lead to next? [Christ's return]

7. What was the *most* important question that Randall asked (this question set the foundation for the future of Mike becoming a Christian)? [Have *you* obeyed the gospel of our Lord?]

8. Notice three critical components of their dialogue:

    a. Randall's question, "*How* were you saved?" He sincerely wanted Mr. Mike to tell the story.

    b. Second, Randall really listened. Listening is a skill that is learned, and it is vital in building human relationships. Can you think of a verse that teaches us the importance of listening? [Jas. 1:19]

    c. Third, Randall continued to question and listen.

9. What final question did Randall ask to invoke the opportunity to have a Bible study? [Don't you need to know what the gospel is and how to obey it?]

10. How did Satan thwart Randall and Michael's Bible study? Research two verses about this strategy of Satan. [gossip]

11. The seed of doubt is compelling. According to the text in the story, what does doubt cause? [Indecision]

Chapter 4:
Yellow Scrap of Paper

November 30, 1987

 1 Peter 3:21

Col. 2:11-13

 ACTION POINTS

1. Continue to memorize one notecard this week.

2. Study 1 Peter 3:21 in its context. How does this verse relate to Colossians 2:11-13?

3. Research the New Testament on the topic of baptism. How many verses are there on the new birth?

4. Consider the fear you feel when thinking about handing someone a scripture scribbled on a piece of paper. What verse helps us manage this fear?

5. Set a goal to introduce yourself to one stranger this week.

Brother and sister, get to work! The work of the disciple is not for the lazy! You've got a lot to do in the next seven days. It's exciting, exhilarating, and a precious opportunity from God! Do not squander your talents or your time. Hey, if this is not for you, find a class that suits you better! If this *is* for you, do not procrastinate. The church of the Lord

Jesus Christ needs courageous sisters and brothers who are ready to begin the Second Restoration Movement.

Yes, you are going to be a part of the Second Restoration Movement! You must be a part of it, because I do not know the people *you* know. Randall does not know the people *you* know. *You* are the only one that can plant the seed into the hearts of those in *your* sphere of influence. Without *you*, they are lost!

Make your list of ten. Review your notecards. Memorize just one card this week. Meet one stranger this week. Study the simple and easy texts recommended. Get excited about your faith! You are about to enjoy an excitement and purpose that you may have never experienced! God has a purpose and plan for your life within the body of Christ.

 DISCUSSION

1. How did Mike become a Baptist?
2. What are the differences in "once saved, always saved" vs. "be thou faithful unto death, and I will give thee a crown of life?"
3. What made Mike think he was a "good guy?"
4. What different course did Randall take after Mike cancelled their Bible study appointment? [handed Mike a Bible verse written on a scrap piece of paper]
5. Larry, Mike's best friend, had started carrying a Bible? Do you know why?
6. What verse did Randall pass off to Michael? [1 Peter 3:21]
7. What did this verse do to Mike? [The verse caused Mike shock, curiosity, and a desire to find out more.]

8. Wouldn't most Christians have given up when Mike cancelled the appointment to study with Randall?

9. How do you feel about Randall handing Mike a verse scribbled on a little piece of note paper?

10. Have *you* ever done this with anyone?

11. Relax. Most of us would never do what Randall did by handing someone a verse on paper. Why? Fear. Fear of rejection, fear of questions, and fear of confrontation. Do you think Randall experienced these same fears?

12. When the company meeting took place and fear of change was created, what was Randall thinking about? [Randall was thinking about ways to reach the lost with the gospel.]

Week II: Chapters 5-8

Spiritually speaking, has it been an incredible past week? How do you feel? The *Action Points Outside of Class* are the key to your Christian growth. What are you here for? Why are you investing your time and effort in this Bible Class? It is about a spiritual payoff. You want to grow beyond who you are today, right?

If you want a life of joy, happiness, and that peace that surpasses all understanding, it takes work. The *Action Points Outside of Class* are a key. **Last week's action points covered a lot of ground.**

Brother and sister, did you want milk or meat? This is meat! Did you think that growth would come easy? We are in spiritual warfare, and it is time we recognize that Satan is seeking to devour us (1 Peter 5:8). Do the work, my brother and sister.

Therefore, my beloved brethren, be ye steadfast, unmovable, always abounding in the work of the Lord, forasmuch as ye know that your labor is not in vain in the Lord.

1 Corinthians 15:58

Chapter 5:
Are They Nuts or What?

December, 1987

 Luke 8:15

 ACTION POINTS

1. Memorize another notecard from your growing stack.
2. Continue to pray for those on your list.
3. Study the book against the text of Ephesians 2:8-9, and see if you draw the same conclusion.
4. Research this dialogue from the book, and note how Randall disarmed Michael and how he treated Michael throughout their discussion.
5. What verse did Randall quote as Mike walked away?

 DISCUSSION

1. Did the Bible discussion go as Mr. Mike had intended? Why?
2. Notice how Randall ended the discussion. What simple teaching did Randall want Mr. Mike to take to bed with him that night? [2 Pet. 3:16]
3. What conclusion did Michael come to at the end of this chapter?

[Eph. 2:8-9 did not support the "faith only" doctrine]

4. Who did Mike turn to for religious advice and instruction? [his Pastor]

5. What was Mike's attitude after receiving advice from the religious expert? [misplaced confidence and arrogance]

6. When Mr. Mike presented his statement to Randall, what was Randall's response? [open, humble, encouraging, patient and willing to examine the scriptures]

7. When Mike called baptism a work, what was Randall's response? [Randall taught Mike the proper context of Eph. 2:8-9]

8. How did Randall "disarm" Mike? [He found something in Mike's response that he could compliment and followed his compliment with encouragement.]

9. How did Satan use the tactic of peer pressure to attempt to thwart Mike's desire to study with Randall? Who was the pressure coming from? [Kirk]

10. Randall began the study from the passages Mr. Mike presented. List the scriptures that Randall presented to guide Mr. Mike into Truth on the topic they were discussing:

    __[2 Tim. 2:15; Eph. 2:8-9; Eph. 2:15; Eph. 2:10-22; Gal. 5:4; Jas. 2:24; 2:17; 2:19; 2 Pet. 3:16; 1 Pet. 4:11]__

11. What *epiphany* did Michael have after Randall teaching him the context of Ephesians 2:8-9?

    [The importance of context and the danger of wresting the scriptures]

12. This was the first "shift" in Mike's mind. When the Truth meets with an honest and good heart, what is the reaction?

13. In your opinion, what did Randall do that impressed Mike the most?

Chapter 6:
Am I Going to Hell?
Later that Morning

Acts 2:47   Col. 1:18

Luke 8:15   Eph. 5:23

ACTION POINTS

1. Continue to memorize another notecard this week.

2. Study the following chart and research the beginning of two of the denominations listed:

Date of Origin (circa)	Name of Group	Originator – Builder	Place of Origin	Books & Creeds Used
33 AD	church, kingdom, house, body, the Way, bride, holy temple of God, habitation of God, assembly	Jesus Christ	Jerusalem	Old and New Testaments (OT/NT)
606 AD	Roman Catholic	Boniface III	Rome	OT with additional seven pseudepigraphal (deuterocanonical) books, NT, and the Catechism of the Catholic Church
1520 AD	Lutheran	Martin Luther	Germany	OT/NT, Book of Concord, and the Handbook of the General Synod (and/or variety of handbooks representing geographical synods)
1534 AD	Church of England/Episcopalian	Henry VIII	England	OT/NT, The Three Creeds, the Nicene Creed, Athanasius's Creed, the Apostles' Creed, Book of Common Prayer, the Clergy and Parish Handbook of the Church of England (and/or a variety of handbooks representing geographical parishes)

1536 AD	Presbyterian	John Calvin	Geneva, Switzerland	OT/NT, Westminster Confession of Faith, the Nicene Creed and the Apostles' Creed
1581 AD	Congregational (Brownists)	Robert Browne	Norwich, England	OT/NT, Savoy Declaration, Declaration of the Faith and Order in Congregational Churches in England, Declaration of the Faith and Order in Congregational Churches in America
1607 AD	Baptist	John Smyth	Amsterdam, Holland	OT/NT, Hiscox Standard Baptist Manual, The New Hiscox Guide for Baptist Churches, and the Standard Manual for Baptist Churches. Some also include the Apostles Creed
1671 AD	Church of God	Stephen Munford	Newport, RI	28 Beliefs of the Church of God, OT/NT
1739 AD	Methodist	John Wesley	England	OT/NT, Nicene Creed, Apostles Creed, General Social Creed and The Book of Discipline of The United Methodist Church

 **DISCUSSION**

1. People outside of the church of Christ commonly state, "That denomination believes they're the only ones going to Heaven." Discuss the many misunderstandings and false perceptions people have about the Lord's church.

2. Is the church of Christ a "denomination?" Discuss the reasons why you think it is or is not. [The church is not a denomination: Denominations are divisions of the original body that Christ gave His blood to purchase (Acts 20:28).]

3. How many arks did Noah build? Was anyone saved outside of the ark (I Peter 3:20-21)?

4. What about the women and children caught in the flood? Do you think any of those who were trying to keep their heads above water prior to drowning in the flood remembered Noah's words and prayed for salvation?

5. How is the Lord's church similar to the ark?

   a. Read out-loud the following verses: Acts 2:47; Col. 1:18; Eph. 4:4; Eph. 5:2.

   b. Does the teaching of the New Testament promote the concept of a singular church (body) or multiple churches (bodies)?

6. What did Kirk say to Mike in his attempt to discourage Mike from discussing the Word with Randall? [Kirk repeated negative gossip disguised in concern and friendship.]

7. What "mantra" confused Mike? [Join the church of your choice.]

8. What scripture refutes this popular mantra? [Acts 2:47]

9. What logical premise did Mike conclude upon? [All denominations teach conflicting doctrines; therefore, it is not possible that all of them are biblically correct.]

10. When Mike pressed Randall for an answer to the question, "Do you think all denominations except yours are going to Hell," what was Randall's three-fold response? In other words, Randall presented at least three responses to avoid answering yes or no. What were they?

    a. _[We are not a denomination.]_

    b. _[I am not the judge of your soul.]_

    c. _[How about we get together tonight and study the Bible?]_

Chapter 7:
Fight or Flight

Later that Morning

 ACTION POINTS

1. Continue memorizing another notecard from your growing stack.

2. Research Luke 8:1-15. What are the four types of soil represented?

    a. ___[hardened]_____

    b. ___[rocky] _____

    c. ___[thorny]_____

    d. ___[fruitful]_____

3. What is the origin of the church of Christ is as found in the Scriptures?

4. Why is it important to know this Bible fact?

5. Do others know about the origin of the church of Christ?

6. When/where do *they think* the church of Christ started?

7. Regarding Dr. Cannon's work relating to his scientific findings that animals react to threats with a general discharge of the sympathetic nervous system, priming the animal for one of two subsequent responses: fighting (fight) or fleeing (flight), how should the Christian react to "spiritual" threats?

8. Randall provided the stimulus for Mike to react according to his spiritual judgment that he was lost. Randall's response initiated his "fight" response.

9. Was this a good or bad thing?

10. How "should" the Christian respond when a person's "fight" mechanism is stimulated by their teaching? Provide two scriptures that confirm your conclusion:

    a. _____

    b. _____

11. In your opinion (from this chapter), what was the most important thing that Randall did that caused Mr. Mike to decide to "search" the scriptures for himself?

12. What verse did Randall quote as Mike walked away?

DISCUSSION

1. Why was Mr. Mike "motivated" to pick up "tracts?" [Randall's opinion that Mike was headed to Hell. His "fight" nature had kicked in. Mike's interest to examine and defend his beliefs that Randall's statement had created.]

2. What affect did these tracts, or picking up these tracts, have on Mike? [The tracts caused Mike to read, to ask questions, and to being to study the Bible alone and with his wife.]

3. What conclusion did he draw from reading the myriad of tracts he collected? [The only "denomination" that seemed able to turn to book, chapter, and verse for everything they believed and practiced was Randall's denomination.]

4. What excellent point did Jonetta bring up regarding "spiritual decisions?" [Regarding spiritual decisions, we are limited to three things: Bible, opinions, and denominational teachings.]

5. What elementary question did Jonetta bring up? [Where did the Baptist Church come from?]

6. How does the knowledge of denominations help us in our effort to seek and save the lost? [Equipping the saints with historical facts that can be used in teaching God's Word.]

Chapter 8:
Enough to Make a Guy Cuss!

Christmas Closing In

Mark 10:24	Luke 12:33	James 1:11
Luke 18:25	Acts 2:44-55	

ACTION POINTS

1. Continue memorizing a notecard from your growing stack.

2. Give any amount you choose to a poor Christian this week.

   a. Note their response. _____

   _____

   b. Note how the act of direct giving made you feel.

   _____

3. Read Luke 21:1-4.

4. Read Acts 4:32-37.

   a. What strikes you about these passages?

   _____

   b. What great sacrifice did Barnabas make?

   _____

DISCUSSION

1. What was Mike's allegation regarding the motivation of today's contemporary churches? [Money, greed, power]

2. According to the LBA, there are currently 297 different Baptist sects around the globe (London Baptist Association, 235 Shaftesbury Avenue, London WC2H 8EP, 2014). With this in mind, it is understandable that not all Baptists believe that John the Baptizer started the Baptist denomination. Do you have any Baptist friends/family? Have you ever asked them of the origin of their particular Baptist sect? Would this be an important question to your Baptist friends/family?

3. In your opinion, do you see any "Christian opulence" within today's church of Christ buildings and/or meeting places?

4. In your opinion, what affect does this have on the body?

5. What affect does it have on the sinner who visits?

6. Consider the following verses:

   a. Mark 10:24

   b. Luke 12:33

   c. Luke 18:25

   d. Acts 2:44-45

   e. James 1:11

7. What were the primary uses of the Christian contribution in the New Testament? Cite at least two references.

   a. _[Acts 2:45, Christians in need]_

   b. _[Acts 4:34, prevented Christian's from lacking what they needed]_

8. Regarding our giving and the distribution of church funds, discuss the differences in how the first-century church utilized contributions as compared to how today's Lord's church utilizes contributions.

9. Is Paul saying in 1 Timothy 5:3-4 that we should remember to give (provide for) to children and parents?

10. While remembering and helping the poor among us, consider Paul's words found in Galatians 6:1-5. What was Paul's concern found in these passages? [Spiritual and emotional needs of the brethren]

11. What is Paul's point in 2 Thessalonians 3:7-15? [The apostle's example of the Christian work ethic, working hard to be self-supportive, and removing the financial motive connected to the gospel.]

Week III: Chapters 9-12

Growing in the Word toward greater Christian maturity takes work doesn't it? Are you getting something out of this class? Please let me remind you again that the *Action Points Outside of Class* are the key in your growth throughout this class.

If you have been doing the Actions Points, do you feel that you are stronger this week than last week? Can you tell that you are growing? At this point you should have a fantastic stack of notecards with Bible verses written on each one. You should be proud of yourself for doing the work; if you have made it this far, I am very proud of you and thankful to God! Keep up the good work!

Trust in the LORD with all thine heart; and lean not unto thine own understanding. In all thy ways acknowledge him, and he shall direct thy paths.

Proverbs 3:5-6

Chapter 9: Lower Than a Pregnant Ant

Later That Afternoon

Romans 5:10

2 Corinthians 5:11

2 Corinthians 5:18

 ACTION POINTS

1. Find the passage in this chapter that demonstrates why people make religious mistakes.

2. Memorize another card from your stack.

3. Take the opportunity to think about someone in your life with whom you have not reconciled. Pray for strength and courage, and then go to that person and make an honest attempt to reconcile with them on the foundation of Matthew 5:23- 24.

4. In this chapter we see one of the many wonderful character traits of Randall, his true nature as defined by the Holy Word of God. How many times have we offended someone, only to later justify and rationalize our actions? Do we live a consistent Christ-like life by following our Lord's instructions found in Matthew 5:23-24 when we offend our family, neighbors, or strangers?

5. Another one of Satan's tactics is to inflame our pride and ego when the need arises to employ Matthew 5:23-24.

6. What prevents you from a total commitment to this foundational principle (assuming you are not totally committed to the principle)?

7. Is there anyone in your life that you have not reconciled with?

8. Consider the following verses.

   a. Romans 5:10

   b. 2 Corinthians 5:11

   c. 2 Corinthians 5:18

 DISCUSSION

1. What affect did Randall's apology have on Mike? [Shame. Mike was ashamed of himself.]

2. How did Randall's actions affect Mike's desire to study the Bible?

3. What primary point did Randall make about the impossibility of John the Baptizer starting the Baptist Church? [John died prior to Christ making the prophecy that He (Christ) would build His church.]

4. What verses did Randall show Mike to teach him about the establishment of Christ's church?

   a. _[Matt. 16:13-18]_

   b. _[Acts 20:28]_

   c. _[Col. 1:18]_

A resource for encouragement: **free** monthly *Muscle and a Shovel e-Newsletter*. It features conversion and restoration stories that are incredibly strengthening to every Christian, young or old! Just go to muscleandashvovel.com and click on the e-Newsletter link.

Chapter 10: Don't Drink the Kool-Aid

Christmas Closing in Fast

Mark 10:24   Luke 12:33   James 1:11

Luke 18:25   Acts 2:44-55   John 3:16

ACTION POINTS

1. Continue memorizing a notecard from your stack.

2. Compare John 3:16 to John 3:1-5

   a. It becomes clear that the word *believe*, in verse 16, is used as a *synecdoche* (si-nek-duh-kee).

   b. Synecdoche is a figure of speech in which a part is used for the whole or the whole for a part.

   c. Example: Bake a cake. The word bake in this example is a part that is used for the whole process, because bake envelops all of the steps required within (grease pan, preheat oven, mix ingredients, cook, remove, ice).

3. Application: Verse 16 says, "*...that whosoever believeth in him should not perish...*" What does the synecdoche "believeth" represent?

 **DISCUSSION**

1. What are some of the many reasons why some think that the church of Christ is a cult?

2. Consider the Lutheran Reverend's inaccuracy of his statement about John 15:5. What are the effects of one misquoted scripture?

3. Randall was now a spiritual fountain for Mike. Name three Christian traits found in the Bible that Randall demonstrated that helped establish him as Mike's "go-to-guy" for spiritual answers? Discuss the power of these principles.

4. Why did Mike remind himself, "Don't drink the Kool-Aid?" [He thought of the possibility that the Lord's church was a cult.]

Chapter 11:
Salt n' Pepper
A Week Before Santa

2 Timothy 3:16-17   Romans 12:18

1 Peter 3:15   Matthew 5:44

 ACTION POINTS

1. Work on memorizing a notecard from that big stack of cards!

2. Consider experiences in your life when you have seen a "Christian" react to negative situations in ways contrary to Christ's teachings found in Matthew 5:44.

3. Consider your own life experiences. Have you ever reacted to a negative event in a way contrary to Matthew 5:44?

4. What can you do to help yourself follow these biblical instructions found in v.44?

 DISCUSSION

1. Have you noticed that Randall stays with small portions of scripture in studying with Mr. Mike? Can we learn something from Randall's method? [People learn by repetitious, small bites]

   a. He maintains the topic at hand.

    b.   He does not dump huge volumes of scripture on Mike during one study.

    c.   He does not try to tell everything he knows all at one time.

2.   Why didn't Randall go through the establishment of the Lord's church, the plan of salvation, the origins of denominationalism, the way New Testament Christians worship, and then invite Mike to his church? [Randall knew that this much information was too much to digest in one lesson. He also disagreed with inviting the "lost" to Christian worship. Instead, Randall believed Jesus' instructions, "*Go ye therefore, and teach all nations, baptizing them in the name of the Father, and of the Son, and of the Holy Ghost: Teaching them to observe all things whatsoever I have commanded you: and, lo, I am with you alway, even unto the end of the world. Amen* (Matt. 28:19-20). He took to heart the command to go, teach, baptize, and then a lifetime of Christian worship to God and the instruction in all things of Christ.]

3.   What did Randall project that was beyond emotional toughness? [Deep patience and love toward his fellow man.]

4.   Discuss how Randall stopped Mike from attacking the man in the diner along with the scripture that Randall quoted. [

5.   What was Randall trying to accomplish in requiring Mike to find the Sinner's Prayer as a "first objective?" [Randall knew that Mike's belief system was built upon the Sinner's Prayer doctrine and that the doctrine did not exist in the Bible.]

Chapter 12:
The Holy Ghost
& the Porch Swing

Christmas at Home

I Corinthians 13:8

1 Corinthians 13:10

  ACTION POINTS

1. Keep working on your notecard. You can do it!
2. Read Acts 2:1-11. What does the word "tongues" mean in this text?
3. Now read 1 Corinthians 12:39 thru 13:13. Paul said, in 12:31, that he would yet show you a more excellent way? What does he mean?
4. How many notecards do you have at this point?

  DISCUSSION

1. What did Aunt Nancy seem to deem more necessary than the Sinner's Prayer? [Receiving the Holy Ghost and manifesting miraculous gifts of the Spirit.]
2. From what you know about tongues, as found in Acts 2:1-11, was Aunt Nancy's "tongue speaking" like that of the those on the Day of Pentecost?

3. What does the Bible require when someone "speaks in tongues?" [1 Cor. 14:27-28]

4. Discuss your thoughts on Mike's questions, "Why do denominations teach opposing doctrines if everyone is going to the same place?" and "How can everyone be religiously correct?"

Week IV: Chapters 13-16

I hope that you are enjoying the study, gaining strength, and being encouraged. This new week will be a lot of fun as we begin with one of my personal favorites – cutting off the end of the ham!

I also hope that the **Action Points** have not overwhelmed you. Jonetta and I realize how busy life can be, and know how difficult it is to juggle family, jobs, bills, errands, appointments, kids, animals, blah, blah, blah!

So, here is a quick word of encouragement for you:

We are more than conquerors through him who loved us. For I am sure that neither death nor life, nor angels nor rulers, nor things present, nor things to come, nor powers, nor height nor depth, nor anything else in all creation, will be able to separate us from the love of God in Christ Jesus our Lord.

Romans 8:37-39

Wow! How incredible is that?

Chapter 13:
Cutting Off the End of the Ham
Last Week of December, 1987

 Proverbs 14:12   Jeremiah 17:9

2 Thessalonians 1:7-8

 ACTION POINTS

1. Yes, you know what I am about to say... memorize another notecard. ☺

2. Asking questions about what we are being taught is a *good* thing. This was the attitude of the Beareans (Acts 17:11).

    a. They received the word with "readiness," but also searched the scriptures every day to verify, validate, and confirm the things they were hearing.

    b. They seemed to have the attitude, "I'm looking forward to hearing this, but I'm going to find out if what I hear is Truth."

    c. Verify something you hear this week with the Word.

3. When you consider your own spiritual condition, have *you* obeyed the gospel? Read Romans 6:1-12 for the Bible's instructions for obeying the gospel.

DISCUSSION

1. Discuss chapter thirteen's bullet points.

2. Why should everyone take great care when following their own heart in religious matters? [The human heart can be deceptive.]

3. What did Mr. Mike begin to see that he did not like as he read the Bible? [The deficiencies of his character, his sins, his materialism, etc.]

4. What was it that caused Mike to *think* that he had found adequate confirmation of his salvation? [The feeling he remembered after saying the Sinner's Prayer.]

Chapter 14:
Feelings... Nothing More Than Feelings

Just a Few Moments Later

Matthew 7:23	John 14:15	Acts 10:34
Matthew 15:9	Romans 6:17	

ACTION POINTS

1. Review your stack of index cards.

2. Google "Your Own Personal Jesus: Is the Language of *a personal relationship* biblical?"

PREFACE TO DISCUSSION: This might be one of the most controversial and provocative chapters in the book. The criticisms received from our brethren regarding this chapter have been surprising, but it has also identified an opportunity for a more in-depth discussion on this topic. I thank you for giving me the latitude within this workbook to offer additional clarity on the contemporary catch-phrase, "Have a personal relationship with Jesus."

Most of us have grown up hearing many in the world of "Christendom" say that they have a personal relationship with Jesus, or that you cannot be saved without having a personal relationship with Jesus. This phrase and the doctrine tied to it was the cornerstone of the popular denominational evangelist, Billy Graham.

Many who profess faith in Christ sincerely desire a relationship with Him. Members of our Lord's church are no different in this respect. Why wouldn't everyone who claims to be a Christian want a personal relationship with Jesus?

While I completely respect the "concept" behind the phrase, the doctrine implied and tied to this phrase does not exist within the pages of the New Testament. Some argue that the "principle" exists, and therefore it is justified and acceptable to God.

I want you to consider an article taken from The Leadership Journal (2006). While I do not like quoting denominational sources, the following should cause us to strongly consider the contemporary denominational doctrine, "have a personal relationship with Jesus." In my opinion, there are statements in this article (excerpts following) that accurately describe the danger and selfishness of the unbiblical doctrine known as the "personal relationship" doctrine.

Your Own Personal Jesus: Is the Language of "A Personal Relationship" Biblical?

In this post, John Suk, a professor of homiletics at Asian Theological Seminary in Manila, The Philippines, challenges popular evangelical jargon by questioning whether having a "personal relationship with Jesus Christ" is poor theology or, worse, a capitulation to therapeutic secular values?

Evangelicals generally insist that "the meaning and purpose of life is to have a personal relationship with Jesus."

We need to do some fundamental reflection on the whole notion of having a "personal relationship" with Jesus Christ. While, on the one hand, I respect the longing for intimacy with God that these words reflect, they also concern me because they betray a creeping sort of secularization of our language about God.

The phrase "a personal relationship with Jesus," is not found in the Bible. Thus, there is no sustained systematic theological reflection on what the phrase means.

As a result, using the language of personal relationship is bound to lead to all sorts of confusion. As a pastor I met more than a few people who experienced doubt, or perhaps anger, because they didn't experience Jesus the way their Christian friends claimed to.

The language of personal relationship with God has become popular due to the pervasive influence of the language of secularity.

*Marsha Witten cogently argues in her book, All is Forgiven: The Secular Message in American Protestantism (Princeton, 1993), Biblical language that emphasizes God's transcendence is replaced by language that emphasizes God's immanence. **Jesus is not in heaven, at the right hand of God; he lives in our hearts. God is primarily seen as a "daddy," as sufferer on our behalf, and as extravagant lover. In these sermons the traditional language for God is accommodated to the human desire for connection and intimacy...** [sermons on having a personal relationship with Jesus] lack much sense that Christianity has anything to say beyond one's personal relationship to God. In both conservative and liberal denominations, **the language*** *of conversion has been replaced by the language of personal relationship. The language of personal relationship fits with secularity; the traditional language of conversion, of trading faiths through a dying to self, does not.*

One cannot fail by recall David Wells' warning:

They labor under the illusion that the God they make in the image of the self becomes more real as he more nearly comes to resemble the self, to accommodate its needs and desires. The truth is quite the opposite. It is ridiculous to assert that God could become more real by abandoning his own character in an effort to identify more completely with ours. And yet the illusion has proved compelling to a whole generation. (God in the Wasteland, Eerdmans, 1994, 100-101.)

Is this possible? Do many Christians have a personal relationship not so much with Jesus, but with something in their heads, with something that they're comfortable with, a social construction driven by their need to go easy on themselves?

In such a world [poverty of the Philippines] I think that rather than focusing on "personal relationship," we need to recover the Psalmist's language of lament because it fairly represents how we ought to feel about Jesus' absence until he comes again to make all things new.

Second, we need to revisit Scripture's assertion that we are "in Christ." Being in Christ, even if it isn't a personal relationship, *is a wonderful and cosmic reality...*

Rather than saying, "I have a personal relationship with Jesus," why don't we say instead, "I have faith in Jesus," or "I believe in Jesus?" Where the language of personal relationship has a very questionable pedigree, amidst a therapeutic culture, to cut God down to a manageable size, the language of faith is deeply rooted in Scripture (emp. MJS).

The apostle John put it this way: "This is [God's] command: to believe in the name of his Son, Jesus Christ, and to love one another as he commanded us" (1 John 3:23).

SOURCE
Leadership Journal, 2006. Pastor & Jethani. Parse: Ministry/Culture. Your Own Personal Jesus; Archives, March 24, 2006

It was the professional baseball player turned evangelist, William "Billy" Sunday, who invented the phrase, *a personal relationship with God* in his 1913 Wilkes-Barre Crusade during what is called the Third Great Awakening. Billy Graham would later modify Sunday's phrase to, "A personal relationship with Jesus Christ."

Why is this important? It is important because this doctrine is man-made, and it did not come into existence until some 1900 years after the New Testament's completion.

Brother and sister, my only prejudice is against teachings that are foreign to God's Word. God has equipped us with the ability to follow Christ's words, *"Thou shalt love the Lord thy God with all thy heart, and with all thy soul, and with all thy mind* (Matt. 22:37)," which goes far beyond any "personal relationship" construct.

DISCUSSION

1. Discuss the power and logic of Randall's "vacation story."

2. What salvation process does the phrase "Have a personal relationship with Jesus" imply? [This doctrine implies and is connected to the doctrine of the Sinner's Prayer, faith alone, and praying for salvation without obedience to God's instructions for salvation.]

3. What did Randall feel from his faith? [Great joy and peace]

4. What was the "key" to Randall's feelings of faith? [Randall's joy and peace was founded upon Truth.]

5. Discuss the power in the points of Saul's conversion.

6. Why was Mr. Mike happier when he was "religiously stupid?" [Ignorance is bliss!]

Chapter 15:
Snake Bite

The Last Few Days of 1987

Hebrews 9:16-17	Galatians 6:2
Ephesians 2:14-16	Romans 6:3-6
John 8:24	Mark 16:15-16
John 12:42	

ACTION POINTS

1. Continue to memorize another notecard this week.

2. Expand your list of ten people to twenty people who have not yet obeyed the gospel. Remember, try your best not to prejudge. Keep this with your stack of notecards.

DISCUSSION

1. Wow! There's a lot in this chapter! We find out that Larry had been studying with Randall and was just baptized. Why do you think Larry hid this from Mike?

2. What does this say about Randall's efforts for the Lord? How many people was Randall studying with? [This is unknown. Mike never found out how many people Randall studied with at any

given time. However, we know that Randall studied with more than one person at a time.]

3. Can you see Randall's teachings coming out in Larry's discussion with Mike?

4. Have you ever considered the aspect that the thief on the cross could not be baptized into Christ because Christ had to first die and be resurrected?

5. Did you notice that Larry covered a lot more biblical ground with Mike in one sitting than Randall did with Mike? Could this be detrimental? If so, why? [Larry was a new Christian and did not know how to study with the lost.]

6. Discuss what Mike said about his reason for being baptized in the Baptist Church.

Chapter 16:
Hot Wings and Aggravation

New Year: 1988

Acts 2:38

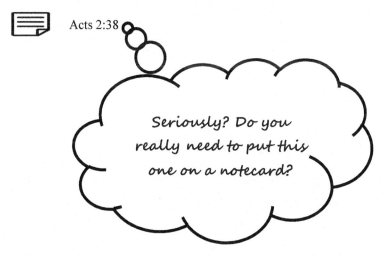

 ACTION POINTS

1. Mike's Approach (try it this week).

    a. Introduce yourself to a stranger. Tell them you are in an evangelism program with a non-denominational church, and you would like to get their opinion of a book.

    b. Tell them that the book is their free gift, but only if they are willing to give you an honest review of the story.

c. If they agree, ask them for a mailing address and an email address. Explain that you will write your cell number in the front cover of the book and ask them to promise to call you when they are finished.

d. Thank them and tell them how excited you are to get their opinion. Say, "You'll love it or hate it – just promise me you'll tell me either way."

a. Do not stand around and wait for them to start questioning, do not try to explain the story, do not try to "sell" or "hype" the story, and do not ask for their "home" address, but rather ask for a mailing address.

2. Here's the typical flow of the conversation:

Mike: "Hey, where you from?"

Prospect: "Anywhere USA"

M: "Great! I ask because I'm in an evangelism program and I need an honest book review. I'll give you the book free *if* you'd give me an honest review. Would you do an honest review – good or bad?"

P: "Yeah, okay, I guess so."

M: "Thanks a lot. Here's my name, address, cell number, and email address. Now, what is a good mailing address for you?"

P: "Just mail it to my office to my attention at 123 Business Avenue, Anywhere, USA."

M: "Could you go ahead and write down your cell number and email address?"

P: "Sure."

M: "Thanks a lot – I'll get it in the mail to you, and I can't wait to hear what you think of it! Would you give me a call when you finish it?"

P: "Yeah, I'll call you when I'm finished."

M: "Thanks again – I'll look forward to hearing from you!"

3. Be upbeat, excited, and smile. If they do not have an interest, do not press them. Just move on to someone else.

4. I keep their information in a calendar, and I note a reminder to call them two weeks after I have shipped the book.

5. Follow up is the key!

6. Does it really work? Ten thousand baptisms have been reported as a result of the book and the power of God's Word. To God be all the glory, credit, honor, and praise!

7. One congregation reported that they are handing them out to the public, free of charge, and one out of every 10 people obey the gospel. That is encouragement!

 DISCUSSION

1. What was the thing that was changing Mike from the inside? [Reading the Bible on a regular basis.]

2. Role-play Mike's Approach (from the previous pages) in class – have fun!

Week V: Chapters 17-20

Has this been fun? Did role-playing make you nervous? Can you imagine how many converts you are going to be responsible for? Teaching others about Jesus Christ and helping others come to the Truth is one of the most satisfying things you can do.

Listen, I do not want to give you the impression that I am trying to get you to buy books. The book just makes things so simple for me, and I truly believe it will be so simple for you too. Giving the book to people is quick, easy, can be done anytime, anywhere. It is a very "low-stress," soft approach, **and it works!**

Each month I set a goal to hand out more books to the lost than the previous month. Ten books is an affordable and effective number, and you can be so flexible with them. I mail it to strangers, leave copies in public places, and put a copy on a friend's doorstep with a note inside.

You probably have better ideas than I do, so please feel free to share your ideas. Do not be afraid to experiment. The thought that you will be teaching and baptizing new disciples is so exciting!

And the LORD, he it is that doth go before thee; he will be with thee, he will not fail thee, neither forsake thee: fear not, neither be dismayed.

Duet. 31:8

Chapter 17:
We Aim to Please
January 1988

 John 12:48   Matthew 7:21
Matthew 15:1

 ACTION POINTS

1. Pray this week with your family on bended knees. It is a wonderful experience.

2. Research the mode of baptism.

3. Oh yeah – memorize another notecard!

 DISCUSSION

1. What verse did Randall quote after Mike told Randall what the Methodist minister had said about the mode of baptism? [Matt. 15:13-14]

2. What did Randall say about people in denominations? [Every denomination has some good people. They teach some truth, and they do some good. Randall was not against the people. He loved their souls. Randall was against false teachings.]

3. Discuss Randall's concern that God will hold people accountable for what they believe and do.

4. If you are married, what can you do *this* week to serve your spouse? If you are not married, what can you do *this* week to serve a friend, family member, or another Christian?

5. Mike and Randall ate a late dinner that Monday night at the office. How does breaking bread with people affect a relationship?

6. Christians in the first century met daily from house to house and ate meals with one another. How often do you meet and eat with Christians?

Chapter 18:
How About Some Cake
January 1988

 Matt. 5:14

 ACTION POINTS

1. Research Transliteration.
2. Continue to memorize another notecard.
3. Review your stack of notecards.

 DISCUSSION

1. Discuss how the word "baptidzo" was transliterated.
2. How were the translators influenced, and thus transliterating the word baptidzo instead of translating the word?
3. To what kind of people will Jesus say, "Depart from Me ye who work iniquity?" (Matt. 7:21-23). Did these people think they were true Christians that were doing the will of God? Why?

Chapter 19:
What's a Eunuch?

Same Evening

Luke 13:3

Acts 8:37

  ACTION POINTS

1. Please work on your notecard (it never hurts to say please).
2. Study the story of the conversion of the Eunuch.
3. What fundamental fact caused Mike to make the decision to leave the Baptist Church?

  DISCUSSION

1. Discuss what our faith is built upon, and what it is not built upon.
2. Why did Mike say that it was easier to get into Heaven than into the Baptist Church? [The Baptist Pastor said that one needed only to believe to go to Heaven, but he had to be voted on and then baptized to get into the Baptist Church.]
3. Discuss what it means to be "on this side of the cross?"
4. When Mike decided to leave the Baptist Church, what concerned followed? [What would mom and dad think?]

5. How does this common concern affect the potential convert and the extended family of the potential convert? [They develop a fear of losing friends and family, a fear of prejudice, and perhaps a fear of persecution. Ask the class to read and discuss this in light of Luke 12:51-53.]

Chapter 20:
Kicked Out of Sunday School

January 10, 1988

1 Tim. 4:1-3	Matt. 23:9	Deut. 30:19
Ezek. 18:20	2 Peter 3:9	Phil. 2:12
Gal. 5:4	Rev. 2:10	1 John 2:2
Titus 2:11-12	Heb. 6:4-6	1 Cor. 9:27
James 1:25	Matt. 24:35	Jo. 17:17
2 Tim. 3:16-17	Gal. 1:8-9	2 Tim. 4:3-4

 ACTION POINTS

1. Complete filling out your notecards through this week – there's a bunch!

 DISCUSSION

1. Discuss why, at this point, Mike thought there were only two options: Catholic or Protestant. [Mike did not yet understand the church of the Bible.]

2. In your opinion, what is the most radical of the five Calvin doctrinal points?

3. Why did the people in the Community Church call Mike a legalist? Discuss legalism and liberalism. [Legalism seeks to bind where the

Bible does not bind. Liberalism seeks to loosen where the Bible does not loosen.]

4. Discuss how New Testament Christians were neither legalists nor liberalists.

5. Discuss the differences between non-denominational and inter-denominational.

Week VI: Chapters 21-24

I have no idea if this material is helping you in your daily life to live for Jesus Christ, nor do I know if you have enjoyed yourself so far. I pray for both!

Count your notecards. You should have around eighty-five at this point in the course. I cannot stress enough how important your notecards are for your growth and Christian success. In my opinion, if you do nothing other than create your Bible notecards, this course will have been worth your time and energy! Keep up your excellent work! Your "season" is coming.

And let us not be weary in well doing: for in due season we shall reap, if we faint not.

Galatians 6:9

Chapter 21:
Muscle and a Shovel
A February Evening 1988

 Matt. 26:28
John 6:68

 ACTION POINTS

1. Find the meaning of the title of this book.

2. Memorize another card from your stack.

3. Expand your list of 20 people to 30 people who have not yet obeyed the gospel. Remember, try your best not to prejudge. Keep this with your stack of notecards

4. Research the mode of baptism.

 DISCUSSION

1. Discuss the meaning of the word "for" in Acts 2:38 (...for the remission...).

2. Discuss the meaning to the weird title of the book, Muscle and a Shovel.

3. Are we willing to dig down deep into the Word? Even when we do not know what we might find? Do we have the type of heart that accepts Truth, regardless of where Truth takes us?

Chapter 22:
Unity Was a Joke!
February 22, 1988

John 17:21   Phil. 2:2

1 Peter 3:8   1 Cor. 1:10-13

ACTION POINTS

1. Research "being of one accord, of one mind."
2. Implement Mike's Approach to one person this week.
3. Continue to memorize a notecard this week.

DISCUSSION

1. We often talk about the many splinter groups found in the denominational world (i.e. the many sects of Baptists). How many different sects are in the body of the Lord (i.e. non-institutional, one cuppers, those who use musical instruments, etc.)?

2. In your opinion what is the cause of the division in the church of Christ?

3. Is our division something that can be repaired? Should it be repaired? Does it even matter? [None of these questions are meant to be controversial or incendiary. They are written with love and with the objective for each Christian to examine the present

condition of the body of Christ. These questions should be answered with complete honesty and with the aim of finding biblical solutions.]

4. How does religious division affect the world's perception of the "Churches in the world of Christendom?" [Lead the class to read Jo. 17:19-21. Consider verse 21, *"That they all may be one; as thou, Father, art in me, and I in thee, that **they also may be one** in us: **that the world may believe** that thou hast sent me."* Unified Christians are "one in us." This type of unity creates belief. Division is not being "one in us," and causes disbelief.]

Chapter 23:
When Momma Ain't Happy
(You know the rest)
Later That Evening

 1 Tim. 6:9

 ACTION POINTS

1. Quote five verses you have memorized from your notecards to a friend or family member without using your cards.

2. Memorize another notecard this week.

 DISCUSSION

1. Discuss the importance of bearing one another's burdens, and the need to be involved with our church family on a daily basis.

2. Discuss those in the church who could use a phone call, a visit, or a card in the mail. [This provides an excellent opportunity for class members to get more involved. Have someone write the names and needs of those mentioned in this discussion.]

3. Who is responsible for maintaining a connection with brothers and sisters in Christ (Elders, Deacons, Minister, members)? [Individual Christians should be involved. This is an opportunity

to discuss the need for each Christian to get involved and stay involved with the body.]

4. Read Acts 2:42-47 again as a group. What would the Lord's church look like today if we continued in the way of our brothers and sisters from verses 42-47? [Daily involvement is the focus of this question.]

Chapter 24:
Why I Didn't Know

February 26, 1988

Jas. 2:24   2 Cor. 11:13-15

Gen. 3:2-4

ACTION POINTS

1. Continue memorizing another card from your stack.

2. Reach out to someone who has not worshipped in a while.

DISCUSSION

1. Discuss the reasons why good people who seem to fear God and believe that Jesus is His Son do not question what they are taught in their respective religions. [They are taught by trusted and loved authority figures. They perceive these figures as knowledgeable. They see others following the same which confirms the teachings in their minds. Additionally, people perceive no need to question due to their "paid professional" status. Time and apathy also play a role.]

2. Discuss examples of how people hear lies repeated constantly until they believe they are facts. [Repetition is the mother of learning.

Hearing a consistent message establishes the message as a "fact" in the human mind.]

3. Discuss the bullet points found in this chapter.

4. Discuss the cunning strategy of Satan brought out in this chapter. [Satan is a highly intelligent being. It is highly probable that his intelligence is far beyond that of any human man or woman. Satan has 6,000 years of experience in deception. He knew that mankind would never follow him openly. Therefore, he mingles small lies with truth. Satan intertwines some good with some twisting of Truth. The core of Satan's strategy is to create confusion, which leads to division. Allow mankind to "think" that he has salvation until his death. Satan attempts to keep good people in biblical ignorance.]

Week VII: Chapters 25-28

This is such an exciting time to be alive. The comforts that we enjoy, the modern medical advancements that sustain and prolong our lives, the technology at our disposal, the ability to network with thousands via digital means, and the opportunities offered to us have never been greater at any other time in human history than it is today.

In Paul's letter to the church at Colossae, he said, *"Which is come unto you, **as it is in all the world**; and bringeth forth fruit, as it doth also in you, since the day ye heard of it, and knew the grace of God in truth* (Col. 1:6)."* In verse 23 he seems to suggest that the gospel had, indeed, been preached to the entire world. He wrote, *"If ye continue in the faith grounded and settled, and be not moved away from the hope of the gospel, which ye have heard, **and which was preached to every creature which is under heaven**; whereof I Paul am made a minister."*

Friend, can the church spread the gospel to the whole world today? There can be no doubt that it can! But remember that it is up to you. You are the hands and feet of Jesus Christ on this earth. God has given you the ability, the tools, and the opportunities to do your individual part. If we each adopt this attitude, nothing can stand in our way. My dear friend, please do not forget:

Have not I commanded thee? Be strong and of a good courage; be not afraid, neither be thou dismayed: for the LORD thy God is with thee whithersoever thou goest.

Joshua 1:9

Chapter 25:
The Church of the Bible

Study 1 of 5 with Randall
February 29, 1988

1 Peter 5:8

Eph. 1:20-23

ACTION POINTS

1. Memorize another card from your stack.

2. Reach out by phone to someone who has not worshipped in a while.

   a. DO NOT tell them they need to come back. They ALREADY know.

   b. Emphasize that they are loved and missed.

   c. Ask them if they are okay, ask what they need, and ask if they are struggling with something.

   d. The last question to always ask is, "What can I do to serve you?"

DISCUSSION

1. Is it a surprise to know that the majority of denominations do not teach, discuss, or have sermons about the church that existed in the New Testament?

2. Discuss how this ignorance and neglect of this topic [the church of the Bible] assists Satan's agenda. [Salvation and being inside the body (church) is one in the same.]

3. Discuss why Mike said that it was easier to get into Heaven than to get into the Baptist Church. [This point was discussed in a past lesson, but is relevant to this portion of the course.]

4. Discuss how it is impossible to teach God's process of salvation without also teaching about the church of the Bible. [Philip preached "Jesus" to the Eunuch, and we find that the Eunuch wanted to be baptized. This is important because we find no teaching of baptism to the Eunuch. Therefore, Philip had to have included the teaching of baptism when he preached Jesus. Additionally, it is baptism that allows God to add the saved to the church (Acts 2:47)].

Chapter 26:
So Many Thoughts

Study 2 of 5

March 1, 1988

Acts 20:7	John 4:24	Matt. 28:19
Col. 3:16	Gal. 3:24	1 Cor. 16:1-2

 ACTION POINTS

1. Keep on memorizing another card from your stack.

2. Visit one elderly member of your congregation.

3. Expand your list of 20 people to 30 people who have not yet obeyed the gospel. Remember, try your best not to prejudge. Keep this with your stack of notecards.

 DISCUSSION

1. Discuss why many denominational people continue to believe that Sunday is the "Sabbath Day." [The root problem is that denominational people are ignorant of the primary dispensations of the Bible. This allows for a "mixing" of Old Testament practices into New Testament practices. This "mixing" opens the door for musical instruments, robes, "priesthood" elevation, tithing, etc.]

2. Discuss why Randall said to Mike, "Mike, there's no command for you anywhere in the New Testament!" [This has been a confusing point for many. Randall's point was to recognize the simple fact that we are reading someone else's mail. The letters were written to a specific audience at a specific time in history. We benefit from these letters since they are the inspired Word of the One True God.]

3. Discuss why many denominations preach the ten percent tithe and your own giving. Do you, on average, give less than ten percent, about ten percent, or more than ten percent?

4. Discuss why the Lord's church does not take a collection through the week, and why we do not do "fund-raisers."

Chapter 27:
What About Music?

Study 3 of 5: March 2, 1988

Eph. 5:18-19   2 Pet. 1:20-21

Gen. 6:14   Lev. 10:1-12

 ACTION POINTS

1. Work on memorizing that notecard.

2. Google the term, "What did New Testament Christians think about music?" It will blow your mind!

3. Again visit one person this week who has not attended services in the past few weeks.

    a. DON'T tell them they need to come back. They ALREADY know.

    b. Emphasize that they are loved and missed.

    c. Ask them if they are okay, ask what they need, and ask if they are struggling with something.

    d. The last question to always ask is, "What can I do to serve you?"

 DISCUSSION

1. Discuss what you found through your Google search (instructions are in the *Action Points*).

2. Discuss how we can help people become more confident in their singing to the Lord.

3. Discuss ways to help our children learn to sing at home, and how we can foster singing together at home during the week. [An effective practice is to make copies of several songs from the song book, and sing them together at home.]

Chapter 28:
Don't Ever Call a Man Reverend?

March 1, 1988: That Afternoon

 Psalms 111:9   Matthew 23:9

Acts 10:26

 ACTION POINTS

1. Verbally quote the Bible verse notecards you have memorized to this point.

 DISCUSSION

1. *Let nothing be done through strife or vainglory; but in lowliness of mind let each esteem other better than themselves* (Phil. 2:3). Discuss lowliness of mind and esteeming others as better than ourselves.

2. What positive affects does your humility and lowliness of mind have on your fellowman? [Question the class on the effects of arrogance and high-mindedness in contrast with humility and lowliness of mind.]

3. Discuss where the word "reverend" is found in scripture and how it is used.

Week VIII: Chapters 29-32

Whoa! This week is jam-packed with lessons and scriptures! Randall has covered some of Mike's most basic arguments against the Truth, and Randall is about to upset the pastoral system Mike had long thought to be from the Bible. In addition, he lays out the gospel of Christ in his "Marshall Keeble" style: interesting, compelling, and with love!

Brother and sister, I pray that you are being filled with excellent spiritual food. However, you might get information constipation!

Moreover, brethren, I would not that ye should be ignorant, how that all our fathers were under the cloud, and all passed through the sea; And were all baptized unto Moses in the cloud and in the sea; And did all eat the same spiritual meat; And did all drink the same spiritual drink: for they drank of that spiritual Rock that followed them: and that Rock was Christ.

1 Corinthians 10:1-4

Chapter 29:
Killing the One-Man Pastoral System

Study 4 of 5 (pushed back): March 3, 1988

Ephesians 4:11	Acts 11:30	Acts 14:23
Titus 1:5	James 5:14	1 Peter 5:1-5

ACTION POINTS

1. Memorize another card from your stack.

2. Expand your list of 30 people to 40 people who have not yet obeyed the gospel. Remember, try your best not to prejudge. Keep this with your stack of notecards. Andrew Gelman, a writer for the New York Times, did an article published in the Times on February 18, 2013. He said that the average American knows 600 people.

3. Give a copy of the book to one person on your list. Explain to them that you are in a Bible class using this tool and would like their honest appraisal (opinion). Ask them for their promise that they will read it beginning to end without jumping around. Then ask them to contact you as soon as they have finished.

DISCUSSION

1. Discuss why the Lord's church doesn't call the preacher a pastor and why. [Lead the class to Eph. 4:11 and discuss the original Greek word *poimen*.]

2. What is the Bible's definition of a pastor? [Wayne Jackson of the Christian Courier offers an excellent study article entitled, "What is a Pastor?" This is an excellent hand-out for the class and can be found at :

https://www.christiancourier.com/articles/1178-what-is-a-pastor]

3. Discuss the dangers in the One-Man Pastoral system. [It is unscriptural and establishes the framework for the abuse of power and corruption. When all authority is given to one man, that man can lead the entire group away from Truth. Discuss the brilliance of God's plan in establishing a plurality of elders to shepherd a local congregation.]

Chapter 30:
The Gospel

Study 4 of 5: March 4, 1988: That Evening

 1 Corinthians 15:1-4

 ACTION POINTS

1. Keep on memorizing another card from your stack.
2. Research the Restoration Pioneers and Alexander Campbell.

 DISCUSSION

1. Discuss all of the bullet points found in the chapter.
2. Discuss the simplicity of the gospel. [1 Cor. 15:1-4]
   a. Discuss the need to re-enact the gospel. [Rom. 6:1-7]
3. Discuss your findings from your research on the Pioneer Preachers of the Restoration Movement.
4. Discuss why we are not Campbellites. [Alexander Campbell was one of many pioneer preachers of the Restoration Movement. When Campbell studied himself into the truth, he began to reject his Baptist doctrines and called for others to become Christians only. This was the beginning of the Baptist hatred for Campbell

and their subsequent labeling of him and those who gladly received what he taught.]

Chapter 31:
Comedic Relief

March 4, 1988: That Evening

 2 Peter 3:9

 ACTION POINTS

1. Keep working on your card from your stack.
2. What is the church? See Matthew 18:20.
3. Why do people say, "Go to church."

 DISCUSSION

1. In your opinion why was Mike fighting against obeying the gospel?
2. Discuss why Mr. Mike thought that God did not want him. [Mike did not believe he could be forgiven. He did not believe that he could successfully repent of his existing sins, and he did not believe he could live a Christian life.]
3. Discuss Mr. Mike's plan to prove to God that God did not want him. [Mike ran to the bottle. What are ways that we each resist God?]

Chapter 32:
That Something

March 10th, 1988: Thursday

 Titus 2:11-12   2 Corinthians 9:7

 ACTION POINTS

1. There's an additional secret method that I use for memorization that I will share with you soon.

2. Memorize the card from your stack.

3. Follow up with those you have given the book to.

4. Recall all of your notecards. See how many you can quote to a friend or family member.

 DISCUSSION

1. Discuss the two options set before men and women, as written in the book. [See bullet points in this chapter.]

2. What was the thing (one word) that was holding Mike back from obeying the gospel? [Pride. It would be a good idea to ask someone in the class to summarize the thoughts of this chapter.]

3. Discuss what reading the Bible did to Mr. Mike. [Reading the Bible opened Mike's eyes and caused him anger and resentment. His anger and resentment was due to the Bible opposing his existing beliefs.]

Week IX: Chapters 33-36

Are you feeling satisfied with this work? Are you feeling more confident in engaging the lost? Have you been following the Action Points? Do you have your notecards completed from the past few weeks? Do you have a list of 40 people that are lost and need the gospel of Jesus Christ? A lot of questions, huh?

I love you and want the best for you. Remember, getting God's Word into your heart and mind takes consistent effort.

The "Conditioning an Elephant" story encapsulates the brotherhood's common problem in their efforts to evangelize.

And Jesus came and spake unto them, saying, All power is given unto me in heaven and in earth. Go ye therefore, and teach all nations, baptizing them in the name of the Father, and of the Son, and of the Holy Ghost: Teaching them to observe all things whatsoever I have commanded you: and, lo, I am with you alway, even unto the end of the world. Amen.

Matthew 28:18-20

Chapter 33:
Conditioning An Elephant

March 11, 1988: Friday

 Romans 12:2   Colossians 1:13

 ACTION POINTS

1. Memorize another card from your stack.
2. Consider the various areas of your life (i.e. work, social, family, spiritual) and ask yourself if you have been mentally conditioned in any of these areas.
3. Is the conditioning positive or negative?
4. How can you improve?

 DISCUSSION

1. Discuss how people become mentally conditioned.
2. Discuss how people shape their lives around a set of beliefs.
3. Discuss how Christians become conditioned regarding sharing the gospel with the lost. [They are afraid. They have a fear of rejection, fear of a confrontation, and fear of a lack of knowledge. They have had negative past experiences.]
4. How can you overcome any mental conditioning in your own life? Awareness is the first step. The second step is positive verbal affirmations. Yes, this sounds weird, but the human mind cannot

overcome a negative thought with a positive thought. The human mind overcomes a negative thought with a positive statement. For example, when one fears the thought of sharing the gospel, they must say out-loud, "I am courageous in sharing the gospel." The third step is the understanding that we alone control our success in overcoming negative mental conditioning.

This is biblical. Proverbs 23:7 says, "*For **as he thinketh in his heart, so is he**: Eat and drink, saith he to thee; but his heart is not with thee.*" Isaiah 26:3 tells us, "*Thou wilt keep him in perfect peace, **whose mind is stayed on thee**: because he trusteth in thee.*" Peter said, "***Wherefore gird up the loins of your mind**, be sober, and hope to the end for the grace that is to be brought unto you at the revelation of Jesus Christ* (1 Peter 1:13)."

God is concerned about how we maintain our thoughts and our minds, and He gives us insight into how to maintain a healthy and confident Christian mind.

5. What tool(s) and values can you use to help someone break through their barriers of mental conditioning? [Positive encouragement is a remarkable thing. Encouragement (edification) is one of the most powerful things we can do for our brethren. Read aloud Gen. 26:24, Exo. 14:13, Matt. 10:31, Acts 27:22.]

Chapter 34:
Just in the Neighborhood
March 12, 1988: Saturday

 1 John 4:7

 ACTION POINTS

1. Work on memorizing the card from your stack.
2. Spend time in prayer. Pray for those on your list. Pray for opportunities to reach those on your list with the gospel.

 DISCUSSION

1. What motivated Randall to stop by and inquire about Mike's Bible study concerns? [1 John 4:7]

2. Discuss how Randall asked many questions and his excellent listening skills. Discuss whether or not we ask questions and actually listen to answers.

3. Do you find it unique, interesting, or strange that Randall asked a final question, listened to the answer, then got up to leave without "pushing" Mike?

4. Discuss the things we learn from the rich man and Lazarus. [After death their positions were fixed. There is no way to change the outcome after death. The rich man remembered his life on earth and his family. He wanted them to be saved from Torments.

Abraham testified to the fact that all must go to and "hear" the Holy Scriptures. Abraham stated in an indirect way that nothing was more powerful than the Bible.]

Chapter 35:
The Last Study

Study 5 of 5: March 14, 1988

1 John 4:4	Rom. 6:22-23	Col. 2:11-13
Acts 2:39	1 Cor. 14:33	Eph. 1:3
John 9:31		

ACTION POINTS

1. Continue to memorize the card from your stack.

2. Please forgive me for repeating this question to you, but have *you* obeyed the gospel? If not, why not?

3. Spend thirty minutes with a Christian this week, and discuss biblical methods to overcome temptation.

DISCUSSION

1. Discuss how Randall taught through asking questions rather than being a "lecturer."

2. What, in your opinion, was Randall's strongest biblical teaching about how baptism washes away sins?

3. Discuss the value of Randall giving Mike "homework" at the close of their study. [The homework assignment kept Mike engaged and active. It would have also given Randall an

opportunity for continued follow up. We must always implement a way for "reconnection" to those we are trying to reach.]

Chapter 36:
Epiphany

March 14, 1988: Monday Night, 11:30 PM

 Rev. 1:16   Hebrews 4:12

Eph. 6:17   1 Tim. 2:3-4

 ACTION POINTS

1. Memorize the card from your stack.

2. Expand your list of 40 people to 50 people who have not yet obeyed the gospel. Remember, try your best not to prejudge. Keep this with your stack of notecards. And congratulations! Your list of 50 is outstanding!

 DISCUSSION

1. Discuss the verse(s) that caused Mike to finally see the Truth. [This was the second time Randall gave Mike a piece of paper with scriptural references. There is power in this approach. The two scriptures that made Mike finally recognize the Truth were John 9:31 and Acts 22:16.]

2. Discuss Jonetta's previous study efforts, her decision, and her actions.

3. Discuss the urgency to be immersed from this chapter in the book, along with the urgency of those in the Bible who responded to the

Truth. [*And that, knowing the time, that now it is high time to awake out of sleep: for now is our salvation nearer than when we believed. The night is far spent, the day is at hand: let us therefore cast off the works of darkness, and let us put on the armour of light* (Rom. 13:11-12)."]

Week X: Chapters 37-40 & Epilogue

Isn't it exciting that you've memorized so many Bible verses? Isn't it thrilling that you have a list of 50 lost souls that you will be able to positively impact with the gospel of Jesus Christ?

I told you of an additional secret method for memorization that I would share later. Later is now! I call it "image anchoring," and it is an easy technique that will allow you to memorize long blocks of scripture. Here is how the technique works.

1. Choose a long section of scriptures that you want to memorize (i.e. Acts 2:37-47).

2. Write or print out the passage on paper with each verse starting on a separate line.

3. Now choose a room in your home. Imagine yourself at the door of that room. In your mind, open the door and look at each item in that room working in a clockwise direction, going from left to right (i.e. door, rocking chair, picture on wall, couch, grandfather clock, window, plant, etc.)

4. Write each item in that room in the left margin next to each scripture (i.e. door v.37; rocking chair v.38; picture on wall v.39; etc.).

5. See the door and memorize that verse. After you have the first verse memorized, repeat the process. See the rocking chair and memorize the next verse.

6. Repeat all of the verses that you have memorized as you work through the list.

7. It takes a little effort, but the payoff is worth it! I am confident that you will be amazed at how easy and powerful this method once it is employed.

*Thy words were found, **and I did eat them; and thy word was unto me the joy and rejoicing of mine heart**: for I am called by thy name, O LORD God of hosts.*

Jeremiah 15:16

Chapter 37:
Digging Down

March 15, 1988: 12:25 AM, Less Than an Hour Later

 John 19:34   Heb. 11:4   Heb. 11:8

Heb. 11:29-31

 ACTION POINTS

1. Memorize another card from your stack.
2. What is the muscle and the shovel as described in the story?
3. Consider the reasons why Truth is so difficult to find in today's world.

 DISCUSSION

1. Discuss why this chapter is titled, "Digging Down."
2. Discuss faith and grace as described in this chapter in the book.
3. Do you agree or disagree with Mike's understanding of faith and grace?
4. What verse did Larry refer to at the end of this chapter? [Romans 8:28]
5. What did Mike mean in his statement, "My spiritual collar had been removed?" [The collar of a lifetime of false teachings.]

Chapter 38:
Top of the Steps
& Into the Water

March 15, 1988: 1:15 AM

Heb. 11:24   John 6:45   2 Cor. 6:17-18

Deut. 30:19

  ACTION POINTS

1. Keep memorizing the card from your stack.

2. Consider the "tone" of the story. What is your honest opinion of Randall?

3. Have you been praying for those on your list, and for opportunities to share the gospel?

  DISCUSSION

1. Discuss the statement made by the one who baptized Mike and Jonetta. Compare this to the following verses:

    a. Ephesians 4:11-15

    b. 2 Corinthians 3:5-6

2. Discuss the scriptural idea that all Christians are ministers and/or priests. Where is this scripture? [1 Pet. 2:9]

Chapter 39:
Sinner's Prayer:
The Greatest Religious Hoax in the History of Mankind

 Rev. 3:15-16   Rom. 10:17   1 Cor. 6:9-10

 ACTION POINTS

1. Memorize another card from your stack.
2. Do you know someone who believes they were saved by the Sinner's Prayer? If yes, take some time to visit with them. Explain to them that you are in a Bible class and doing research on the Sinner's Prayer. Ask them to share their "salvation experience" with you.

 DISCUSSION

1. Discuss the fact that good, sincere, honest, moral, God-fearing, Jesus-believing people truly believe that the Sinner's Prayer comes from the Bible, even though it does not.
2. Discuss how we can approach and help these good people with true love in our hearts for their souls.
3. Discuss the bullet points found in this chapter. [It is important to note that many Christians, especially those who were baptized at a

young age, know that baptism is important. However, they may not necessarily know the efficacies of baptism. These are outlined in the bullet points. It is very important to discuss these points with the class.]

Chapter 40:
Yes, It *Is* About You

 Gal. 1:8-9   Heb. 9:27

 ACTION POINTS

1. Continue to memorize a card from your stack.
2. Consider this chapter's title. What is meant by the title?

 DISCUSSION

1. Discuss what is meant by this chapter's title.
2. Discuss how false doctrines have proliferated through time as stated in this chapter.
3. Discuss the challenge issued in this chapter. [The challenge is to get out your shovel and dig. Read the Word for yourself, and find whether or not the things presented in this story are true as compared to the Word.]
4. Are we being "negative" by discussing what is true and what is false?
   a. Why are some of our brethren "turned off" when discussing these issues?
   b. Discuss the need for balance.

Epilogue
Randall's Secret

 Luke 8:1-7   Luke 8:8-15

 ACTION POINTS

1. Keep memorizing a card from your stack.

2. Now you know Randall's secret! You have been doing it throughout this course! Consider how his method has helped you.

3. Will _**you**_ become a Randall?

 DISCUSSION

1. Discuss how the Lord's will gets into our hearts. [Memorizing imprints the Word onto the human heart.]

2. Discuss your current level of desire, zeal, and commitment to the Lord, and what you believe you can achieve in sharing the gospel. [This should be an exciting activity, and you, the instructor, should be excited when discussing the possibilities. Enthusiasm breeds enthusiasm!]

3. Discuss your fears and concerns. [Do NOT let this become the dominant class topic of discussion.]

4. Discuss how you can help one another overcome these fears and concerns. Remember that Jesus sent them out in pairs. Discuss why it is so important to have a friend or companion in your evangelistic efforts. [Have the class take notes when discussing ways to overcome fears and concerns. Each person's ideas may help another in overcoming their own personal fears and concerns.]

Week XI: Motive & Growth

 2 Cor. 6:8

 ACTION POINTS

1. Memorize another card from your stack.
2. Research how Christians gave (i.e. free will, voluntary, as they were prospered, cheerfully)
3. Research what the saint's contributions were used for.

 DISCUSSION

Discuss the following: [Read the following out loud]

May I take a moment to tell you how much my family and I appreciate you? We truly do. Even though we do not know each other, it is important to us that you know that we pray for you. We pray for all of our brothers and sisters in Christ.

We appreciate you because of your willingness to study this course. We appreciate you because of your great support of this humble work. We appreciate you because you love the Lord and *you want* to make a difference for eternity.

Everyone who knows me can verify that I have a deep concern in respect to "making merchandise" of my brethren (2 Peter 2:1-3). I fear this greatly, which is why I refuse the idea of taking books to speaking and preaching engagements. This is also why I do not take any "fees" for speaking and preaching. The profits we earn from this work go back into this ministry effort, and we thank you for enabling and supporting this work!

Again, may we give all glory to God, for without God and the resurrection of His Son Jesus Christ, we are the most pitiful people? Paul said, *"For if the dead rise not, then is not Christ raised: And if Christ be not raised, your faith is vain; ye are yet in your sins. Then they also which are fallen asleep in Christ are perished. If in this life only we have hope in Christ, we are of all men most miserable* (1 Cor. 15:16-19)."

With this being said, it is vitally important to the Shank family that you know that we are not trying to "peddle" a book. The book, *Muscle and a Shovel*, is simply a tool. It's intended to be a tool to:

1. Help you grow in your faith.
2. Edify and build up the body of Christ.
3. Promote Truth.
4. Open the eyes of the lost to doctrines not found in the Bible.
5. Be a way for you to easily and quickly reach the perishing.

It is with *this* thought and motive that we press forward. I would suggest the following "next steps" for your growth, and for the growth of the kingdom of Christ.

1. At this point you should have approximately 168 notecards in your stack, and you should have memorized approximately twelve cards! Excellent job! God bless you for writing the Word onto your heart!
2. Pray for the 50 lost souls on your list.
3. Consider your own best approach.

a. Open Bible study

b. Gospel video presentation

c. Jule Miller Video Presentation & Workbooks

d. Tracts

e. World Video Bible School videos (hundreds of topics)

f. Fishers of Men Program

g. Bible correspondence courses

h. Internet and email

i. Muscle and a Shovel (of course I'm going to say it!)

I have experimented with all of the approaches listed above. There are pros and cons with *every* method and approach. Our time, in today's world, is very limited, and there's no single approach that works for everyone.

You see, we are just like you. We work *more* than full-time, we're trying to raise a family, trying to maintain a home, and unfortunately the "busy-ness" of this life chokes out our ability to spend 10-15 hours every week in "one-on-one" Bible studies. And to you mother's, we truly understand.

However, it takes me about a minute a day to give away a book! My individual goal is to give away a book a day. This method fits our busy lifestyles, while sowing the seeds of the gospel, correcting religious error, revealing Truth, and calling the reader to action.

It's the most "no-pressure" approach that we've found, and the only pressure comes from Randall and the Word. However, this is only our opinion, and it is not intended to make you feel like this is the best approach. It may not be the best approach. Additionally, I am **_not_** telling *you* to give away a book a day, or to give away *any at all. Your* method of sowing the gospel seed must fit *your* personality, lifestyle, budget, and time constraints. I'm simply sharing what we try to do.

[Please emphasize that this is only my opinion and is not meant to be binding, nor is it meant to cause any strife or controversy.] Let me share something with you that I am excited about. One of the best things the Lord's church can do to is to remove the "Ego Board." What is the Ego Board? The Ego Board is the board that every congregation has hanging on the wall in the auditorium. It displays attendance and contribution numbers.

What is wrong with hanging and maintaining this board?

1. It is not scriptural.

2. The apostles were not focused on attendance numbers, visitors, and the contribution.

3. It causes undue stress on the congregation because their zeal oscillates as the weekly numbers change (i.e. stress when low and excitement when high).

If we could get every congregation to remove the Ego Board and, instead, post the weekly numbers of Christians sowing the gospel seed, you would begin to see members stepping forward to sow the seed.

If we removed the contribution amount and, instead, posted how much money went to poor Christians and money spent on spreading the gospel, the focus would change quickly and dramatically.

If we focused on brethren sowing seed, and giving to the Christian poor and needy, the body of Christ would once again be aligned with the Word of God and with a proper scriptural focus. It would have a leadership with a vision of true New Testament growth, and a congregation that utilizes the weekly financial gifts in the same way the first century church used free will offerings in the first century.

Brothers and sisters, Jesus Christ wants us to sow the gospel seed. **We are to sow seeds everywhere we go,** and the Word of God will do the rest! Amen?

Week XII: Second Restoration Movement

 Romans 16:16

 ACTION POINTS

1. Memorize another card from your stack.

2. Research the New Testament and find the passages that teach about growth:

   a.   How was growth achieved in the first century?

   b.   What hasn't the Lord's church grown today like it did in the first century?

   c.   Do not be discouraged. The Lord's church can and will grow as it did in the first century. It takes vision, faith, and a simple plan. I'll give you the vision and simple plan on the next few pages.

 DISCUSSION

[Read the following out loud. Discuss the potential for growth.] Many congregations are having great success using *Muscle and a Shovel* to sow the seeds of the kingdom. I am finding that many individuals give away 10 books each month. Here's an example email from a brother in Christ:

Subject: Muscle And A Shovel Success Story
Date: Mon, 7 Jul 2014 20:49:27
From: Will Crump <@outlook.com>
To: Michael J Shank <jonettashank@gmail.com>

Hi Mike and Jonetta!

The North Jackson Church of Christ has been giving away copies of your book to the public and 1 in 10 are obeying the Gospel from reading the book! [One of the ladies at church shared this in a Bible class a while back. The North Jackson congregation is located at 2870 U.S. 45 Bypass, Jackson, TN, 38305. Their website is http://www.northjacksonchurchofchirst.com].

Thought you'd like to hear of the good your book is doing.

Yours in Christ,

Will Crump
Bolivar church Of Christ
(Used with the written permission of Will Crump via email)

If the North Jackson congregation is experiencing a "1 in 10 lost souls obeying the gospel ratio" from this humble work, to God be all the glory! We have received a variety of reports stating that between 1 and 6 to 1 in 20 were obeying the gospel after reading the book; however, it is impossible to know. Furthermore, it should be noted that much depends on the receptiveness of the people in a particular area, as well as how well the brethren follow up with those they give the book to.

At any rate, this knowledge caused me to think about the possibilities of a Second Restoration Movement. On the next few pages you will find a simple example of the potential that exists for a Second Restoration Movement using one congregation of 50 people over a six month period of time using the 1 of 10 obeying the gospel ratio. Here is a vision for the future:

THE LORD'S CHURCH NEEDS A FORWARD VISION: SOWING THE SEEDS FOR 6 MONTHS

EXAMPLE: MONTH 1

A congregation with an attendance of:	50
Number of Christians who sow with Muscle:	10
Copies given away by each Christian:	10
Number of new souls reached:	100
1 in 10 obey the gospel:	10
Kingdom expanded to:	60

EXAMPLE: MONTH 2

The 10 original Christians sowing with Muscle and the 10 newly converted sow with Muscle = 20 sowers

Congregation expanded to:	60
Number of Christians who sow with Muscle:	20*
Copies given away by each Christian:	10
Number of new souls reached:	200
1 in 10 obey the gospel:	20
Kingdom expanded to:	80

EXAMPLE: MONTH 3

The 20 sowers from month 2 and the 20 new converts sowing with Muscle = 40 sowers

Congregation expanded to: 80

Number of Christians who sow with Muscle: 40*

Copies given away by each Christian: 10

Number of new souls reached: 400

1 in 10 obey the gospel: 40

Kingdom expanded to: 120

EXAMPLE: MONTH 4

The 40 sowers from month 3 and the 40 new converts sowing with Muscle = 80 sowers

Congregation expanded to: 120

Number of Christians who sow with Muscle: 80*

Copies given away by each Christian: 10

Number of new souls reached: 800

1 in 10 obey the gospel: 80

Kingdom expanded to: 200

EXAMPLE: MONTH 5

The 80 sowers from month 4 and the 80 new converts sowing with Muscle = 160 sowers

Congregation expanded to: 200

Number of Christians who sow with Muscle: 160*

Copies given away by each Christian: 10

Number of new souls reached: 1600

1 in 10 obey the gospel: 160

Kingdom expanded to: 360

EXAMPLE: MONTH 6

The 160 sowers from month 5 and the 160 new converts sowing with Muscle = 320 sowers

Congregation expanded to: 360

Number of Christians who sow with Muscle: 320*

Copies given away by each Christian: 10

Number of new souls reached: 3200

1 in 10 obey the gospel: 320

Kingdom expanded to: **680**

From fifty to 680 in six months! Can you imagine the excitement, joy, love, and refreshment that would come with the Lord adding these to the body? This is first century Christianity. We find that when the Word of the Lord increases, the kingdom increases! *"And the word of God increased; and the number of the disciples multiplied in Jerusalem greatly; and a great company of the priests were obedient to the faith* (Acts 6:7)."

Remember, in this example, the congregation started with 50 people; however, 40 decided to do nothing and 10 decided to sow the seed of the gospel to 10 new souls each month. The same 40 continued to do nothing throughout the example. Only the original 10 Christians and *all* of the new converts sowed the seed to 10 new souls each month.

Why would the new converts be willing to sow the seed? Do you remember what it was like when you became a Christian? Do you remember the excitement that you felt? And do you remember how you wanted to share the good news with your friends and family?

It is *usually* during this time in the new convert's life when they are the most excited and the most willing to take the Truth to their friends and family. Think about the woman at the well? *The woman then left her water pot, and went her way into the city, and saith to the men, Come, see a man, which told me all things that ever I did: is not this the Christ? Then they went out of the city, and came unto him* (John 4:28-30). Brother and sister, this is further evidence that *you can* make a difference.

How many people has Randall touched with the gospel? How many souls - entire families – will his effort with one man make for eternity? What if Randall had been too afraid, too busy, or too apathetic to have given me a loving hand, a couple of doughnuts, and the simple statement, "I might even have something better for you a little later?"

This is the impact of *one* man. Randall. One humble, kind, patient, zealous Christian with an act of kindness and a simple statement.

Brother and sister in Christ, I am nothing special. I am an average, everyday guy trying my best to live our faith, and trying to encourage others to do the same. I fail, I make mistakes, and I commit sin, and come short of the glory of God. If this confession shocks you, please forgive me, but if I say I have no sin I lie and the truth is not in me.

So you see, the power is not in me. The power is not in *any* man, nor in *any* man-made work like *Muscle and a Shovel*. **The power is in the sowing of the seed – the sowing of the magnificent work of ultimate power and complete perfection which is God's Holy Word, a Word that shall never pass away** (Matt. 24:35). This begs the question, "How can we sow the seed in the fastest and most effective way?"

The key is *you*. Brother and sister, *you can* make a difference. *You can be a Randall.* The original question stands. *Will you be a Randall?* Someone's soul is depending on *you* at this very moment!

Week XIII:

 Read through all of your notecards. You should be thrilled by this great accomplishment.

 ACTION POINTS

1. Memorize another card from your stack – NO! Just kidding! If you've made it this far, you've done terrific!

 DISCUSSION

1. Each person in class quotes one verse they have memorized.

2. Discuss your confidence level today as compared to your confidence level at the beginning of this class.

3. Discuss the impact that the memorization has had on your confidence and in your Christian life.

4. Discuss the most important thing you have gleaned from this class.

5. Discuss the evangelistic approach that best suits you, your personality, your lifestyle, and your time constraints.

6. Last thing – get out there and sow the seed! God go with you, my friend. [Thank you, teacher!]

THANK YOU

A very special note of appreciation goes to Christa Bryant. Christa is a wonderful Christian and an excellent editor:

Christa,

Thank you so much for your valuable time and willingness to edit this work. May our Lord bless you and your family throughout eternity.

Your Brother with Christian Love,

Mike

If you need professional editing work, I highly recommend Christa Bryant. Her contact information is below:

Christa M. Bryant

1302 Clark Brothers Drive

Buda, Texas 78610

christamsb@yahoo.com

ORDERING INFORMATION

The retail price of this Teacher's Manual, and the Bible Class Student Workbook, is $9.95 per copy. You can get these titles direct from the author for $5.97 per copy (40% discount) at:

muscleandashovel.com

You can also order from Amazon.com, Barnes & Noble, Books-a-Million, Ingram Books, The Book Depository, and many Christian bookstores across the nation.

We hope you'll consider signing up for the free *Muscle and a Shovel Newsletter*. The newsletter features conversion and restoration stories of those who've read *Muscle and a Shovel*. You can sign up at the author's website listed above.

We would also sincerely invite you to post your comments on the Muscle and a Shovel Facebook page.

Thanks so much!

Mike

Michael Shank

Spanish Translation

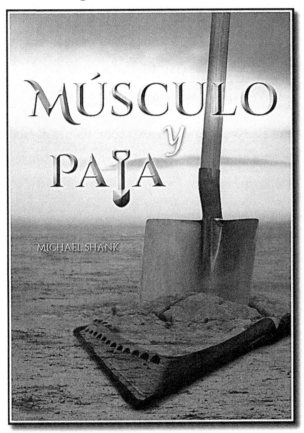

We are also thrilled to announce the release of *Muscle and a Shovel* in Spanish! God be glorified for the opportunity to reach our Hispanic friends and neighbors with the gospel of Jesus Christ!

The Spanish version has been professionally edited and formatted by Brother Moisés Pinedo. It is an edition that you will proud to use in your evangelistic efforts.

The retail price of the Spanish translation is $15.95. You can purchase a single copy for $14.95, or multiple copies at multi-copy volume discounts for evangelistic efforts from the author at:

muscleandashovel.com

Find us on Facebook at:

https://www.facebook.com/pages/Muscle-and-a-Shovel/225178630892427

God bless your every effort to reach the lost and perishing. May our Lord be glorified and may the kingdom expand with every tribe and tongue around the globe.

PUBLICATIONS

Muscle and a Shovel, 6th Edition Revised (*professionally edited, chapter titles removed, offensive words removed*)

Muscle and a Shovel Hardback, 6th Edition Revised (*professionally edited, chapter titles removed, offensive words removed*)

Muscle and a Shovel Bible Class Student Workbook

Muscle and a Shovel Spanish translation

PUBLICATIONS PENDING

Muscle and a Shovel Portuguese translation

Muscle and a Shovel Russian translation

Muscle and a Shovel Chinese translation

Muscle and a Shovel Large Print version

Muscle and a Shovel Audio version

CPSIA information can be obtained at www.ICGtesting.com
Printed in the USA
BVOW06s0333110416

443197BV00008B/65/P